FAMOUS PRAYERS

Abingdon Press

Famous Prayers

Copyright © 1987 by Abingdon Press

All rights reserved.

ISBN 0-687-12784-X

Unless otherwise indicated all Scripture quotations in this publication are from the Holy Bible, New International Version. Copyright © 1973, 1978, 1984, International Bible Society.

Scripture quotations noted (KJV) are from the King James Version of the Bible.

The prayers of Soren Kierkegaard on page 39 are from the book *The Prayers of Kierkegaard.* Used by permission of the University of Chicago Press.

MANUFACTURED BY THE PARTHENON PRESS AT
NASHVILLE, TENNESSEE, UNITED STATES OF AMERICA

Preface

From earliest times, people have communicated with God through prayer. In these pages are prayers from the Old Testament, the New Testament, and great Christians throughout the centuries.

Over the centuries the themes remain constant: thanksgiving, petition, confession of sin, anger and confusion, fear, love and gratitude, vows, longing, intercession, praise.

This collection presents only a taste of the great wealth of prayerful expressions to be found in the history of the Bible and the Christian faith. May it stir new vigor in your own prayer life and perhaps lead you to explore the historic prayers of Christianity further.

The Spirit helps us in our weakness. We do not know what we ought to pray for, but the Spirit himself intercedes for us with groans that words cannot express (Rom. 8:26).

Contents

Old Testament Prayers... 7
New Testament Prayers... 15
Christian Prayers Through the Centuries... 20
Personal Prayers.. 42
Author Index.. 47
Subject Index... 48

OLD TESTAMENT PRAYERS

Melchizedek's Blessing of Abraham
Genesis 14:19-20

"Blessed be Abram by God Most High,
   Creator of heaven and earth.
And blessed be God Most High,
   who delivered your enemies into your hand."

Abraham's Intercession for Sodom
Genesis 18:23-32

Then Abraham approached him and said: "Will you sweep away the righteous with the wicked? What if there are fifty righteous people in the city? Will you really sweep it away and not spare the place for the sake of the fifty righteous people in it? Far be it from you to do such a thing—to kill the righteous with the wicked, treating the righteous and the wicked alike. Far be it from you! Will not the Judge of all the earth do right?"

The Lord said, "If I find fifty righteous people in the city of Sodom, I will spare the whole place for their sake."

Then Abraham spoke up again: "Now that I have been so bold as to speak to the Lord, though I am nothing but dust and ashes, what if the number of the righteous is five less than fifty? Will you destroy the whole city because of five people?"

"If I find forty-five there," he said, "I will not destroy it."

Once again he spoke to him, "What if only forty are found there?"

He said, "For the sake of forty, I will not do it."

Then he said, "May the Lord not be angry, but let me speak. What if only thirty can be found there?"

He answered, "I will not do it if I find thirty there."

Abraham said, "Now that I have been so bold as to speak to the Lord, what if only twenty can be found there?"

He said, "For the sake of twenty, I will not destroy it."

Then he said, "May the Lord not be angry, but let me speak just once more. What if only ten can be found there?"

He answered, "For the sake of ten, I will not destroy it."

Jacob's Vow
Genesis 28:20-22

"If God will be with me and will watch over me on this journey I am taking and will give me food to eat and clothes to wear so that I return safely to my father's house, then the Lord will be my God and this stone that I have set up as a pillar will be God's house, and of all that you give me I will give you a tenth."

Moses' Prayer for Guidance
Exodus 33:13

I pray thee, if I have found grace in thy sight, shew me now thy way, that I may know thee, that I may find grace in thy sight: and consider that this nation is thy people. (KJV)

Moses' Prayer for Pardon
Exodus 34:9

If now I have found grace in thy sight, O Lord, let my Lord, I pray thee, go among us; for it is a stiffnecked people; and pardon our iniquity and our sin, and take us for thine inheritance. (KJV)

Moses' Prayer to See the Promised Land
Deuteronomy 3:24-25

O Lord God, thou hast begun to shew thy servant thy greatness, and thy mighty hand: for what God is there in heaven or in earth, that can do according to thy works, and according to thy might?

I pray thee, let me go over, and see the good land that is beyond Jordan, that goodly mountain, and Lebanon. (KJV)

Firstfruits Prayer
Deuteronomy 26:5-10

A Syrian ready to perish was my father, and he went down into Egypt, and sojourned there with a few, and became there a nation, great, mighty, and populous:

And the Egyptians evil entreated us, and afflicted us, and laid upon us hard bondage:

And when we cried unto the Lord God of our fathers, the Lord heard our voice, and looked on our affliction, and our labour, and our oppression:

And the Lord brought us forth out of Egypt with a mighty hand, and with an outstretched arm, and with great terribleness, and with signs, and with wonders:

And he hath brought us into this place, and hath given us this land, even a land that floweth with milk and honey.

And now, behold, I have brought the firstfruits of the land, which thou, O Lord, hast given me. And thou shall set it before the Lord thy God, and worship before the Lord thy God. (KJV)

Hannah's Vow for the Unborn Samuel
I Samuel 1:11

O Lord of hosts, if thou wilt indeed look on the affliction of thine handmaid, and remember me, and not forget thine handmaid, but wilt give unto thine handmaid a man child, then I will give him unto the Lord all the days of his life, and there shall no razor come upon his head. (KJV)

David's Confession
II Samuel 24:10b

I have sinned greatly in that I have done: and now, I beseech thee, O Lord, take away the iniquity of thy servant; for I have done very foolishly. (KJV)

Solomon's Prayer for Wisdom
I Kings 3:7-9

"O Lord my God, you have made your servant king in place of my father David. But I am only a little child and do not know how to carry out my duties. Your servant is here among the people you have chosen, a great people, too numerous to count or number. So give your servant a discerning heart to govern your people and to distinguish between right and wrong. For who is able to govern this great people of yours?"

Solomon's Prayer of Dedication of the Temple
I Kings 8:26-30

"And now, O God of Israel, let your word that you promised your servant David my father come true.

"But will God really dwell on earth? The heavens, even the highest heaven, cannot contain you. How much less this temple I have built! Yet give attention to your servant's prayer and his plea for mercy, O Lord my God. Hear the cry and the prayer that your servant is praying in your presence this day. May your eyes be open toward this temple night and day, this place of which you said, 'My Name shall be there,' so that you will hear the prayer your servant prays toward this place. Hear the supplication of your servant and of your people Israel when they pray toward this place. Hear from heaven, your dwelling place, and when you hear, forgive."

Solomon's Blessing of Israel
I Kings 8:56-61

"Praise be to the Lord, who has given rest to his people Israel just as he promised. Not one word has failed of all the good promises he gave through his servant Moses. May the Lord our God be with us as he was with our fathers; may he never leave us nor forsake us. May he turn our hearts to him, to walk in all his ways and to keep the commands, decrees and regulations he gave our fathers. And may these words of mine, which I have prayed before the Lord, be near to the Lord our God day and night, that he may uphold the cause of his servant and the cause of his people Israel according to each day's need, so that all the peoples of the earth may know that the Lord is God and that there is no other. But your hearts must be fully committed to the Lord our God, to live by his decrees and obey his commands, as at this time."

Praise
Psalm 3:3-4

But thou, O Lord, art a shield for me; my glory, and the lifter up of mine head.
I cried unto the Lord with my voice, and he heard me out of his holy hill. Selah. (KJV)

Praise
Psalm 9:1-2

I will praise you, O Lord, with all my heart;
   I will tell of all your wonders.
I will be glad and rejoice in you;
   I will sing praise to your name, O Most High.

Thanks for Comfort
Psalm 23:4-5

Yea, though I walk through the valley of the shadow of death, I will fear no evil: for thou art with me; thy rod and thy staff they comfort me.

Thou preparest a table before me in the presence of mine enemies: thou anointest my head with oil; my cup runneth over. (KJV)

Thanks
Psalm 30

I will extol thee, O Lord; for thou has lifted me up, and hast not made my foes to rejoice over me.

O Lord my God, I cried unto thee, and thou hast healed me.

O Lord, thou hast brought up my soul from the grave: thou has kept me alive, that I should not go down to the pit.

Sing unto the Lord, O ye saints of his, and give thanks at the remembrance of his holiness.

For his anger endureth but a moment; in his favour is life: weeping may endure for a night, but joy cometh in the morning.

And in my prosperity I said, I shall never be moved.

Lord, by thy favour thou hast made my mountain to stand strong: thou didst hide thy face, and I was troubled.

I cried to thee, O Lord; and unto the Lord I made supplication.

What profit is there in my blood, when I go down to the pit? Shall the dust praise thee? shall it declare thy truth?

Hear, O Lord, and have mercy upon me: Lord, be thou my helper.

Thou has turned for me my mourning into dancing: thou has put off my sackcloth, and girded me with gladness;

To the end that my glory may sing praise to thee, and not be silent. O Lord my God, I will give thanks unto thee for ever. (KJV)

For Refuge
Psalm 31:1-5

In you, O Lord, I have taken refuge;
    let me never be put to shame;
    deliver me in your righteousness.
Turn your ear to me,
    come quickly to my rescue;
be my rock of refuge,
    a strong fortress to save me.
Since you are my rock and my fortress,
    for the sake of your name lead and guide me.
Free me from the trap that is set for me,
    for you are my refuge.
Into your hands I commit my spirit;
    redeem me, O Lord, the God of truth.

Praise
Psalm 36:5-10

Thy mercy, O Lord, is in the heavens; and thy faithfulness reacheth unto the clouds.

Thy righteousness is like the great mountains; thy judgments are a great deep: O Lord, thou preservest man and beast.

How excellent is thy lovingkindness, O God! therefore the children of men put their trust under the shadow of thy wings.

They shall be abundantly satisfied with the fatness of thy house; and thou shalt make them drink of the river of thy pleasures.

For with thee is the fountain of life: in thy light shall we see light.

O continue thy lovingkindness unto them that know thee; and thy righteousness to the upright in heart. (KJV)

An Individual Lament
Psalm 42

As the hart panteth after the water brooks, so panteth my soul after thee, O God.

My soul thirsteth for God, for the living God: when shall I come and appear before God?

My tears have been my meat day and night, while they continually say unto me, Where is thy God?

When I remember these things, I pour out my soul in me: for I had gone with the multitude, I went with them to the house of God, with the voice of joy and praise, with a multitude that kept holyday.

Why art thou cast down, O my soul? and why art thou disquieted in me? hope thou in God: for I shall yet praise him for the help of his countenance.

O my God, my soul is cast down within me: therefore will I remember thee from the land of Jordan, and of the Hermonites, from the hill Mizar.

Deep calleth unto deep at the noise of thy waterspouts: all thy waves and thy billows are gone over me.

Yet the Lord will command his lovingkindness in the daytime, and in the night his song shall be with me, and my prayer unto the God of my life.

I will say unto God my rock, Why hast thou forgotten me? why go I mourning because of the oppression of the enemy?

As with a sword in my bones, mine enemies reproach me; while they say daily unto me, Where is thy God?

Why art thou cast down, O my soul? and why art thou disquieted within me? hope thou in God: for I shall yet praise him, who is the health of my countenance, and my God. (KJV)

For Guidance
Psalm 139:23-24

Search me, O God, and know my heart: try me, and know my thoughts:
And see if there be any wicked way in me, and lead me in the way everlasting. (KJV)

Jeremiah's Lament
Jeremiah 15:15-18

You understand, O Lord;
    remember me and care for me.
    Avenge me on my persecutors.
You are long-suffering—do not take me away;
    think of how I suffer reproach for your sake.
When your words came, I ate them;
    they were my joy and my heart's delight,
for I bear your name,
    O Lord God Almighty.
I never sat in the company of revelers,
    never made merry with them;
I sat alone because your hand was on me
    and you had filled me with indignation.
Why is my pain unending
    and my wound grievous and incurable?
Will you be to me like a deceptive brook,
    like a spring that fails?

Jeremiah's Complaint
Jeremiah 20:7

O Lord, you deceived me, and I was deceived;
    you overpowered me and prevailed.
I am ridiculed all day long;
    everyone mocks me.

Gratitude for Deliverance
Lamentations 3:54b-58

I am cut off.
I called upon thy name, O Lord, out of the low dungeon.
Thou hast heard my voice: hide not thine ear at my breathing, at my cry.
Thou drewest near in the day that I called upon thee: thou saidst, Fear not.
O Lord, thou has pleaded the causes of my soul; thou has redeemed my life. (KJV)

Daniel's Prayer of Praise
Daniel 2:20-22

Blessed be the name of God for ever and ever: for wisdom and might are his:

And he changeth the times and the seasons: he removeth kings, and setteth up kings: he giveth wisdom unto the wise, and knowledge to them that know understanding:

He revealeth the deep and secret things: he knoweth what is in the darkness, and the light dwelleth with him. (KJV)

NEW TESTAMENT PRAYERS

PRAYERS OF JESUS

The Lord's Prayer
Matthew 6:9-13

Our Father which art in heaven, Hallowed be thy name.
Thy kingdom come. Thy will be done in earth, as it is in heaven.
Give us this day our daily bread.
And forgive us our debts, as we forgive our debtors.
And lead us not into temptation, but deliver us from evil: For thine is the kingdom, and the power, and the glory, for ever. Amen. (KJV)

At the Raising of Lazarus
John 11:41b-42

"Father, I thank you that you have heard me. I knew that you always hear me, but I said this for the benefit of the people standing here, that they may believe that you sent me."

High Priestly Prayer
John 17:1-19

"Father, the time has come. Glorify your Son, that your Son may glorify you. For you granted him authority over all people that he might give eternal life to all those you have given him. Now this is eternal life: that they may know you, the only true God, and Jesus Christ, whom you have sent. I have brought you glory on earth by completing the work you gave me to do. And now, Father, glorify me in your presence with the glory I had with you before the world began.

"I have revealed you to those whom you gave me out of the world. They were yours; you gave them to me and they have obeyed your word. Now they know that everything you have given me comes from you. For I gave them the words you gave me and they accepted them. They knew with certainty that I came from you, and thy believed that you sent me. I pray for them. I am not praying for the world, but for those you have given me, for they are yours. All I have is yours, and all you have is mine. And glory has come to me through them. I will remain in the world no longer, but they are still in the world, and I am coming to you. Holy Father, protect them by the power of your name—the name you gave me—so that they may be one as we are one. While I was with them, I protected them and kept them safe by that name you gave me. None has been lost except the one doomed to destruction so that Scripture would be fulfilled.

"I am coming to you now, but I say these things while I am still in the world, so that they may have the full measure of my joy within them. I have given them your word and the world has hated them, for they are not of the world any more than I am of the world. My prayer is not that you take them out of the world but that you protect them from the evil one. They are not of the world, even as I am not of it. Sanctify them by the truth; your word is truth. As you sent me into the world, I have sent them into the world. For them I sanctify myself, that they too may be truly sanctified."

At Gethsemane
Matthew 26:39

"My Father, if it is possible, may this cup be taken from me. Yet not as I will, but as you will."

On the Cross
Luke 23:34, 43, 46

Father, forgive them; for they know not what they do. . . .
Verily I say unto thee, To-day shalt thou be with me in paradise. . . .
Father, into thy hands I commend my spirit. (KJV)

Matthew 27:46

Eli, Eli, la-ma sa-bach-tha-ni? that is to say, My God, my God, why hast thou forsaken me? (KJV)

OTHER NEW TESTAMENT PRAYERS

At the Birth of the Messiah
Luke 2:14

Glory to God in the highest, and on earth peace, good will toward men. (KJV)

Prayer of Simeon
Luke 2:29-32

Lord, now lettest thou thy servant depart in peace, according to thy word:
For mine eyes have seen thy salvation,
Which thou hast prepared before the face of all people;
A light to lighten the Gentiles, and the glory of thy people Israel. (KJV)

Prayer for Peter and John
Acts 4:24b-30

"Sovereign Lord, . . . you made the heaven and the earth and the sea, and everything in them. You spoke by the Holy Spirit through the mouth of your servant, our father David:

" 'Why do the nations rage
    and the peoples plot in vain?
The kings of the earth take their stand
    and the rulers gather together
against the Lord
    and against his Anointed One.'

Indeed Herod and Pontius Pilate met together with the Gentiles and the people of Israel in this city to conspire against your holy servant Jesus, whom you anointed. They did what your power and will had decided before hand should happen. Now, Lord, consider their threats and enable your servants to speak your word with great boldness. Stretch out your hand to heal and perform miraculous signs and wonders through the name of your holy servant Jesus."

The Publican's Prayer
Luke 18:13

God be merciful to me a sinner. (KJV)

The Dying Thief's Prayer
Luke 23:42

"Jesus, remember me when you come into your kingdom."

Stephen's Dying Prayer
Acts 7:60a

"Lord, do not hold this sin against them."

Paul's Conversion Prayer
Acts 22:10

"What shall I do, Lord?"

Paul's Prayer for the Church at Ephesus
Ephesians 3:14-21

    For this reason I kneel before the Father, from whom his whole family in heaven and on earth derives its name. I pray that out of his glorious riches he may strengthen you with power through his Spirit in your inner being, so that Christ may dwell in your hearts through faith. And I pray that you, being rooted and established in love, may have power, together with all the saints, to grasp how wide and long and high and deep is the love of Christ, and to know this love that surpasses knowledge—that you may be filled to the measure of all the fullness of God.
    Now to him who is able to do immeasurably more than all we ask or imagine, according to his power that is at work within us, to him be glory in the church and in Christ Jesus throughout all generations, for ever and ever! Amen.

Paul's Prayer to the Corinthians
II Corinthians 1:3-5

Praise be to the God and Father of our Lord Jesus Christ, the Father of compassion and the God of all comfort, who comforts us in all our troubles, so that we can comfort those in any trouble with the comfort we ourselves have received from God. For just as the sufferings of Christ flow over into our lives, so also through Christ our comfort overflows.

Prayer for the Coming of Jesus
Revelation 22:20b

Amen. Come, Lord Jesus.

CHRISTIAN PRAYERS THROUGH THE CENTURIES

FOR JOY AND GLADNESS
The Clementine Liturgy
First Century

Blessed art Thou, O Lord, who hast nourished me from my youth up, who givest food to all flesh. Fill our hearts with joy and gladness, that we, always having all sufficiency in all things, may abound to every good work in Christ Jesus our Lord, through whom to Thee be glory, honour, might, majesty, and dominion, forever and ever. Amen.

FOR ALL KINGS AND RULERS
Clement of Rome
First Century

Grant unto all Kings and Rulers, O Lord, health, peace, concord, and stability, that they may administer the government which Thou hast given them without failure. For Thou, O heavenly Master, King of the Ages, givest to the sons of men glory and honour, and power over all things that are upon the earth. Do Thou, Lord, direct their counsel according to that which is good and well pleasing in Thy sight, that administering in peace and gentleness, with godliness, the power which Thou hast given them, they may obtain Thy favour. O Thou Who alone art able to do these things, and things far more exceeding good than these, for us, we praise Thee, through the High Priest and Guardian of our souls Jesus Christ; through Whom be the glory and the majesty, unto Thee, both now and for all generations, and forever and ever. Amen.

FOR STEWARDSHIP
Barnabas
Second Century

O Lord God Almighty, who hast built Thy Church upon the foundation of the Apostles, under Christ the head corner-stone, and to this end didst endue Thy holy apostle St. Barnabas with the singular gift of the Holy Ghost; leave me not destitute, I humbly beseech Thee, of Thy manifold gifts and talents, nor yet of grace to make a right use of them always without any sordid self-ends, to Thy honour and glory; that, making a due improvement of all those gifts Thou graciously entrustest me with, I may be able to give a good account of my stewardship when the great Judge shall appear, the Lord Jesus Christ, who reigneth with Thee and the Eternal Spirit, one God, blessed forever. Amen.

PRAYER FOR GOD'S HELP
Irenaeus
Second Century

Give perfection to beginners, O Father; give intelligence to the little ones; give aid to those who are running their course. Give sorrow to the negligent; give fervour of spirit to the lukewarm. Give to the perfect a good consummation; for the sake of Christ Jesus our Lord. Amen.

PRAYER TO THE TEACHER
Clement of Alexandria
Second Century

Be gracious, O Instructor, to us Thy children, Father, Charioteer of Israel, Son and Father, both in One, O Lord. Grant to us who obey Thy precepts, that we may perfect the likeness of the image, and with all our power know Him who is the good God and not a harsh judge. And do Thou Thyself cause that all of us who have our conversation in Thy peace, who have been translated into Thy commonwealth, having sailed tranquilly over the billows of sin, may be wafted in calm by Thy Holy Spirit, by the ineffable wisdom, by night and day to the perfect day; and giving thanks may praise, and praising thank thee Alone Father and Son, Son and Father, the Son, Instructor and Teacher, with the Holy Spirit, all in One, in whom is all, for whom all is One, for whom is eternity, whose members we all are, whose glory the aeons are; for the All-good, All-lovely, All-wise, All-just One. To whom be glory both now and forever. Amen.

MORNING PRAYER
The Eastern Church
Third Century

We give thee hearty thanks for the rest of the past night, and for the gift of a new day, with its opportunities of pleasing thee. Grant that we may so pass its hours in the perfect freedom of thy service, that at eventide we may again give thanks unto thee; through Jesus Christ our Lord. Amen.

PRAYERS OF AUGUSTINE
For Light and Guidance
Fourth Century

O God our Father, who dost exhort us to pray, and who dost grant what we ask, if only, when we ask, we live a better life; hear me, who am trembling in this darkness, and stretch forth Thy hand unto me; hold forth Thy light before me; recall me from my wanderings; and, Thou being my Guide, may I be restored to myself and to Thee, through Jesus Christ. Amen.

For Perseverance

I know, O Lord, and do with all humility acknowledge myself an object altogether unworthy of Thy love; but sure I am, Thou art an object altogether worthy of mine. I am not good enough to serve Thee, but Thou hast a right to the best service I can pay. Do Thou then impart to me some of that excellence, and that shall supply my own want of worth. Help me to cease from sin according to Thy will, that I may be capable of doing Thee service according to my duty. Enable me so to guard and govern myself, so to begin and finish my course, that, when the race of life is run, I may sleep in peace, and rest in Thee. Be with me unto the end, that my sleep may be rest indeed, my rest perfect security, and that security a blessed eternity. Amen.

Take My Heart!

Take my heart! for I cannot give it Thee:
Keep it! for I cannot keep it for Thee.

For Hope

O Lord our God, under the shadow of Thy wings let us hope. Thou wilt support us, both when little, even to gray hairs. When our strength is of Thee, it is strength; but, when our own, it is feebleness. We return unto Thee, O Lord, that from their weariness our souls may rise towards Thee, leaning on the things which Thou hast created, and passing on to Thyself, who hast wonderfully made them; for with Thee is refreshment and true strength. Amen.

Delight in God's Praise

Thou awakest us to delight in Thy praises; for Thou madest us for Thyself, and our heart is restless, until it repose in Thee.

Te Deum Laudamus
Church Liturgy

We praise thee, O God: we acknowledge thee to be the Lord. All the earth doth worship thee: the Father everlasting. To thee all Angels cry aloud: the Heavens, and all the Powers therein.
To thee Cherubim and Seraphim: continually do cry,
Holy, Holy, Holy: Lord God of Sabaoth;
Heaven and earth are full of the Majesty: of thy Glory.
The glorious company of the Apostles: praise thee.
The goodly fellowship of the Prophets: praise thee.
The noble army of Martyrs: praise thee.
The holy Church throughout all the world: doth acknowledge thee;
The Father: of an infinite Majesty;
Thine honourable, true: and only Son;
Also the Holy Ghost: the Comforter.

Be Thou My Vision

Be thou my Vision, O Lord of my heart;
Naught be all else to me, save that thou art;
Thou my best thought, by day or by night,
Waking or sleeping, thy presence my light.

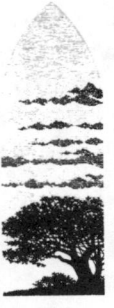

CHRIST, BE WITH ME
St. Patrick
Fifth Century

Christ, be with me, Christ before me, Christ behind me,
Christ in me, Christ beneath me, Christ above me,
Christ on my right, Christ on my left.
Christ when I lie, Christ when I sit, Christ where I arise,
Christ in the heart of every one who thinks of me,
Christ in the mouth of every one who speaks of me,
Christ in every eye that sees me,
Christ in every ear that hears me.
    Salvation is of the Lord,
    Salvation is of the Lord,
    Salvation is of the Christ,
    May your salvation, O Lord, be ever with us.

DELIGHT IN CHRIST
Bernard of Clairvaux (Ascribed)
Twelfth Century

Jesus, Thou joy of loving hearts!
    Thou fount of life! Thou light of men!
From the best bliss that earth imparts,
    We turn unfilled to Thee again.

Thy truth unchanged hath ever stood;
    Thou savest those that on Thee call;
To them that seek Thee, Thou art good,
    To them that find Thee—All in All!

We taste Thee, O Thou living bread,
    And long to feast upon Thee still;
We drink of Thee, the fountain head,
    And thirst our souls from Thee to fill.

Our restless spirits yearn for Thee,
    Where'er our changeful lot is cast;
Glad, when Thy gracious smile we see,
    Blest, when our faith can hold Thee fast.

O Jesus, ever with us stay!
    Make all our moments calm and bright
Chase the dark night of sin away—
    Shed o'er the world Thy holy light! Amen.

AH! SWEET JESUS
Bonaventura
Thirteenth Century

Ah! sweet Jesus, pierce the marrow of my soul with the healthful shafts of Thy love, that it may truly burn, and melt, and languish, with the only desire of Thee; that it may desire to be dissolved, and to be with Thee; let it hunger alone for the bread of life: let it thirst after Thee, the spring and fountain of eternal light, the stream of true pleasure; let it always desire Thee, seek Thee, and find Thee, and sweetly rest in Thee. Amen.

DAILY PRAYER OF THOMAS AQUINAS
Thomas Aquinas
Thirteenth Century

Grant me, I beseech Thee, O merciful God, prudently to study, rightly to understand, and perfectly to fulfill that which is pleasing to Thee, to the praise and glory of Thy name.

Thou, O Christ, art the King of glory; Thou art the everlasting Son of the Father. Amen.

DAILY PRAYER OF FRANCIS OF ASSISI
Francis of Assisi
Thirteenth Century

My God, and my all, who art Thou, sweetest Lord, my God? And who am I, a poor worm, Thy servant? Holiest Lord, I would love Thee! Sweetest Lord, I would love Thee! Lord, my God, I give to Thee all my heart and body, and vehemently desire, if I might know how, to do more for Thy love. Amen.

MAKE ME AN INSTRUMENT OF THY PEACE
Francis of Assisi

Lord, make me an instrument of Thy peace;
Where hate rules, let me bring love,
Where malice, forgiveness,
Where disputes, reconciliation,
Where error, truth,
Where doubt, belief,
Where despair, hope,
Where darkness, Thy light,
Where sorrow, joy!

O Master, let me strive more to comfort others than
    to be comforted,
To understand others than to be understood,
To love others, more than to be loved!

For he who gives, receives,
He who forgets himself, finds,
He who forgives, receives forgiveness,
And dying, we rise again to eternal life. Amen.

FOR THY SPIRIT
Michelangelo
Fifteenth Century

The prayers I make will then be sweet indeed,
If Thou the spirit give by which I pray;
My unassisted heart is barren clay,
That of its native self can nothing feed;
Of good and pious works Thou art the seed
That quickens only where Thou say'st it may.
Unless Thou show to us Thy own true way,
No man can find it! Father! Thou must lead;
Do Thou then breathe those thoughts into my mind
By which such virtue may in me be bred
That in Thy holy footsteps I may tread;
The fetters of my tongue do Thou unbind,
That I may have the power to sing to Thee,
And sound Thy praises everlastingly! Amen.

PRAYER FOR FRIENDS
Thomas à Kempis
Fifteenth Century

Almighty, everlasting God, have mercy on Thy servants our friends. Keep them continually under Thy protection, and direct them according to Thy gracious favour in the way of everlasting salvation; that they may desire such things as please Thee, and with all their strength perform the same. And forasmuch as they trust in Thy mercy, vouchsafe, O Lord, graciously to assist them with Thy heavenly help, that they may ever diligently serve Thee, and by no temptations be separated from Thee; through Jesus Christ our Lord. Amen.

AN INTERCESSORY PRAYER
Thomas à Kempis

I offer up unto Thee my prayers and intercessions, for those especially who have in any matter hurt, grieved, or found fault with me, or who have done me any damage or displeasure.

For all those also whom, at any time I may have vexed, troubled, burdened, and scandalized, by words or deeds, knowingly or in ignorance; that Thou wouldst grant us all equally pardon for our offences against each other.

Take away from our hearts, O Lord, all suspiciousness, indignation, wrath, and contention, and whatsoever may hurt charity, and lessen brotherly love.

Have mercy, O Lord, have mercy on those that crave Thy mercy, give grace unto them that stand in need thereof, and make us such as that we may be worthy to enjoy Thy grace, and go forward to life eternal. Amen.

PRAYER FOR CONSOLATION AND SUPPORT
Thomas à Kempis

O Thou most sweet and loving Lord, Thou knowest mine infirmities, and the necessities which I endure; in how great evils and sins I am involved; how often I am weighed down, tempted, and disturbed by them. I entreat of Thee consolation and support. I speak to Thee who knowest all things, to whom all my inward thoughts are open, and who alone canst perfectly comfort and help me. Thou knowest what things I stand in most need of. Behold, I stand before Thee poor and naked, calling for grace, and imploring mercy. Refresh Thy hungry supplicant, kindle my coldness with the fire of Thy love, enlighten my blindness with the brightness of Thy presence. Suffer me not to go away from Thee hungry and dry, but deal mercifully with me, as often times Thou has dealt wonderfully with Thy saints. Amen.

GIVE ME GRACE
Thomas More
Sixteenth Century, written several weeks before his execution, July 7, 1535

Give me thy grace, good Lord,
To set the world at nought,
To set my mind fast on thee.
And not to hang upon the blast of men's mouths.
To be content to be solitary,
Not to long for world company,
Little and little utterly to cast off the world,
And rid my mind of all the business thereof.
Gladly to be thinking of God,
Piteously to call for his help,
To lean upon the comfort of God,
Busily to labor to love him.

GRACE TO LABOUR
Thomas More

The things, good Lord, that we pray for, give us the grace to labour for.

FOR CHARITY
Thomas More

And give me, good Lord, an humble, lowly, quiet, peaceable, patient, charitable, kind and filial and tender mind, every shade, in fact, of charity, with all my words and all my works, and all my thoughts, to have a taste of thy holy blessed Spirit.

FOR UNITY IN BODY AND MIND
Coverdale
Sixteenth Century

O merciful God, grant us love, that we seek not our own honor, but the profit of our neighbor and thy glory in all things. Expel out of us all disdain, greediness, ungentleness, headiness, and flattering of ourselves. Preserve us from discord and division; bind us together in uniform love; that we may be one body, and of one mind. Establish also our faith, that our minds may be always comforted in the resurrection of thy Son, and immortal life purchased by him. Amen.

TEACH ME TO BE GENEROUS
Ignatius of Loyola
Sixteenth Century

Dearest Lord, teach me to be generous;
Teach me to serve thee as thou deservest;
To give and not to count the cost,
To fight and not to heed the wounds,
To toil and not to seek for rest,
To labour and not to seek reward,
Save that of knowing that I do thy will.

BURIAL OF THE DEAD
Orthodox

Blessed is the path thou goest on this day, for a place of rest is prepared for thee.

PRAYERS OF LUTHER
Morning Prayer
Sixteenth Century

We give thanks unto thee, heavenly Father, through Jesus Christ thy dear Son, that thou hast protected us through the night from all danger and harm; and we beseech thee to preserve and keep us, this day also, from all sin and evil; that in all our thoughts, words, and deeds, we may serve and please thee. Into thy hands we commend our bodies and souls, and all that is ours. Let thy holy angel have charge concerning us, that the wicked one have no power over us. Amen.

For Greater Spirituality

Behold, Lord, an empty vessel that needs to be filled. My Lord, fill it. I am weak in the faith; strengthen thou me. I am cold in love; warm me and make me fervent that my love may go out to my neighbor. I do not have a strong and firm faith; at times I doubt and am unable to trust thee altogether. O Lord, help me. Strengthen my faith and trust in thee. In thee I have sealed the treasures of all I have. I am poor; thou art rich and didst come to be merciful to the poor. I am a sinner; thou art upright. With me there is an abundance of sin; in thee is the fulness of righteousness. Therefore, I will remain with thee of whom I can receive but to whom I may not give. Amen.

A Child's Prayer

Ah, dearest Jesus, Holy Child,
Make thee a bed, soft, undefiled,
Within my heart, that it may be
A quiet chamber kept for thee.

On Prayer

Lord, thou knowest that I do not presume to come before thee of myself nor on account of my worthiness. Were I to rely on my merits,* I could not lift up mine eyes unto thee, and would not know how to begin to pray. But I come because thou thyself hast commanded and dost earnestly request that we should call upon thee, and hast promised to hear us. Thou hast also sent thine only Son who has taught us what we shall pray and has even spoken the words we shall say. Hence, I know that this prayer is pleasing to thee. However great my boldness to consider myself a child of God in thy presence may seem to be, I must yield to thee for thou wilt have it thus. I would not accuse thee of falsehood, and thus adding to my sins offend thee still more by despising thy command and doubting thy promise. Amen.

---

*"on this"

For Peace

In these our days so perilous,
Lord, peace in mercy send us;
No God but thee can fight for us,
No God but thee defend us;
    Thou our only God and Savior.

For Faith

  O God, where would we be if thou shouldest forsake us? What can we do if thou withdrawest thy hand? What can we know if thou never enlightenest? How quickly the learned become babes; the prudent, simple; and the wise, fools! How terrible art thou in all thy works and judgments! Let us walk in the light while we have it, so that darkness may not overcome us. Many renounce their faith and become careless and weary of thy grace. Deceived by Satan into thinking they know everything and have no need, they feel satisfied and thus become slothful and ungrateful, and are soon corrupted. Therefore, help us to remain in the ardor of faith that we may daily increase in it through Jesus Christ our real and only Helper. Amen.

PRAYERS OF CALVIN
Evening Prayer
Sixteenth Century

O Lord God, who hast given man the night for rest, as thou hast created the day for his work, we beseech thee to give our bodies a night of rest that our minds may awake to thee and our hearts be always full of thy love. Let us never forget thee, O Lord, nor thy goodness. Let the remembrance of thy mercy be always engraven on our minds. Grant that our sleep may not be an indulgence but only serve to strengthen us that we may be more alert in thy service. Be pleased to keep us chaste in body and mind and safe from all temptations and dangers, that our sleep may turn to the glory of thy name. But since this day has not passed away without our having in many ways offended thee through our proneness to evil, just as all things are now covered by the darkness of the night, so, O Lord, let everything that is sinful in us lie buried in thy mercy. Through Jesus Christ, our Savior. Amen.

For Continued Obedience

Almighty God, as thou hast hitherto shown to us so many favors since the time thou hast been pleased to adopt us as thy people, O grant that we may not forget so great a kindness. May we not be led away by the allurements of Satan, nor seek for ourselves inventions, which may at length turn to our ruin. May we instead continue fixed in our obedience to thee, and daily call on thee, and drink of the fulness of thy bounty, and at the same time strive to serve thee from the heart, and to glorify thy name. Thus may we prove that we are wholly devoted to thee, according to the great obligation under which thou hast laid us, when it pleased thee to adopt us in thine only-begotten Son. Amen.

For Imitation of Christ

Almighty God, inasmuch as thou hast been pleased to set before us an example of every perfection in thine only-begotten Son, grant that we may study to form ourselves in imitation of him. May we follow not only what he has prescribed, but also what he performed, that we may truly prove ourselves to be his members, and thus confirm our adoption. May we so proceed in the whole course of our life that we may at length be gathered into that blessed rest which the same, thine only-begotten Son, hath obtained for us by his own blood. Amen.

Good Works

Grant, almighty God, since thou art pleased kindly to invite us to thyself, and hast consecrated thy Word for our salvation, that we may willingly, and from the heart, obey thee, and become teachable. May we be so planted in the courts of thine house, that we may grow and flourish, and that fruit may appear through the whole course of our life, until we shall at length enjoy that blessed life which is laid up for us in heaven, through Christ our Lord. Amen.

RELIANCE ON GOD
John Donne
Seventeenth Century

O Lord,
never suffer us to think
that we can stand by ourselves,
and not need thee.

PRAYER FOR THE SOUL
John Donne

Eternal and most glorious God, suffer me not so to undervalue myself as to give away my soul, Thy soul, Thy dear and precious soul, for nothing; and all the world is nothing, if the soul must be given for it. Preserve therefore, my soul, O Lord, because it belongs to Thee, and preserve my body because it belongs to my soul. Thou alone dost steer my boat through all its voyage, but hast a more especial care of it, when it comes to a narrow current, or to a dangerous fall of waters. Thou hast a care of the preservation of my body in all the ways of my life; but, in the straits of death, open Thine eyes wider, and enlarge Thy Providence towards me so far that no illness or agony may shake and benumb the soul. Do Thou so make my bed in all my sickness that, being used to Thy hand, I may be content with any bed of Thy making. Amen.

FOR THOSE DEPARTED
Book of Common Prayer

We bless Thy holy name for all Thy servants departed this life in Thy faith and fear; beseeching Thee to give us grace so to follow their good examples, that with them we may be partakers of Thy heavenly kingdom. Grant this, O Father, for Jesus Christ's sake, our only Mediator and Advocate. Amen.

FOR THOSE WHO MOURN
Book of Common Prayer

Almighty God, Father of all mercies and giver of all comfort: Deal graciously, we pray thee, with those who mourn, that casting every care on thee, they may know the consolation of thy love; through Jesus Christ our Lord.

PRAYERS OF WESLEY
Fix Then Our Steps
Eighteenth Century

Fix Thou our steps, O Lord, that we stagger not at the uneven motions of the world, but steadily go on to our glorious home, neither censuring our journey by the weather we meet with, nor turning out of the way for anything that befalls us.

In Thy Service

Thou art never weary, O Lord, of doing us good. Let us never be weary of doing thee service. But, as thou hast pleasure in the prosperity of thy servants, so let us take pleasure in the service of our Lord, and abound in thy work, and in thy love and praise evermore. O fill up all that is wanting, reform whatever is amiss in us, perfect the thing that concerneth us. Let the witness of thy pardoning love ever abide in all our hearts.

For the Spirit's Liberty

Deliver me, O God, from too intense an application to even necessary business. I know the narrowness of my heart and that an eager attention to earthly things leaves it no room for the things of heaven. Teach me to go through all my employments with so truly disengaged a heart that I may still see thee in all things, and that I may never impair that liberty of spirit which is necessary for the love of thee.

For a Lively Spirit

Deliver me, O God, from a slothful mind, from all lukewarmness and all dejection of spirit. I know these cannot but deaden my love to thee; mercifully free my heart from them, and give me a lively, zealous, active, and cheerful spirit, that I may vigorously perform whatever thou commandest and be ever ardent to obey in all things thy holy love.

Thanks for the Eucharist

Whither, O my God, should we wander if left to ourselves? Where should we fix our hearts if not directed by thee?

Thou didst send forth thy Holy Spirit to guide and comfort us, and give thyself in the Holy Eucharist to feed and nourish our hungry souls with that sacramental food.

Still thou art really present to us in that holy mystery of love; hence we offer up our devotions in it with our utmost reverence, wonder, and love.

For Holiness

Cure us, O thou great Physician of souls, of all our sinful distempers.
Cure us of this intermitting piety, and fix it into an even and a constant holiness.
Oh, make us use religion as our regular diet and not only as a medicine in necessity.
Make us enter into a course of hearty repentance and practice virtue as our daily exercise.
So shall our souls be endued with perfect health and disposed for a long, even for an everlasting, life.

JESUS, LOVER OF MY SOUL
Charles Wesley
Eighteenth Century

Jesus, lover of my soul,
Let me to thy bosom fly,
While the nearer waters roll,
While the tempest still is high:
Hide me, O my Savior, hide,
Till the storm of life is past;
Safe into the haven guide;
O receive my soul at last!

PRAYER
John Keble
Nineteenth Century

Only, O Lord, in Thy dear love
Fit us for perfect rest above;
And help us this and every day,
To live more nearly as we pray.

FOR PEACE
John Henry Newman
Nineteenth Century

O Lord, support us all the day long of this troublous life, until the shadows lengthen, and the evening comes, and the busy world is hushed, and the fever of life is over, and our work is done. Then, in Thy great mercy, grant us a safe lodging, and a holy rest, and peace at the last; through Jesus Christ our Lord. Amen.

STAY WITH ME
John Henry Newman

Stay with me, and then I shall begin to shine as thou shinest: so to shine as to be a light to others. The light, O Jesus, will be all from thee. None of it will be mine. No merit to me. It will be thou who shinest through me upon others. O let me thus praise thee, in the way which thou dost love best, by shining on all those around me. Give light to them as well as to me; light them with me, through me. Teach me to show forth thy praise, thy truth, thy will. Make me preach thee without preaching—not by words, but by my example and by the catching force, the sympathetic influence, of what I do—by my visible resemblance to thy saints, and the evident fulness of the love which my heart bears to thee.

EVER A CHILD
John Henry Newman

Thou, O my God, art ever new, though thou art the most ancient—thou alone art the flood for eternity. I am to live for ever, not for a time—and I have no power over my being; I cannot destroy myself, even though I were so wicked as to wish to do so. I must live on, with intellect and consciousness for ever, in spite of myself. Without thee eternity would be another name for eternal misery. In thee alone have I that which can stay me up for ever: thou alone art the food of my soul. Thou alone art inexhaustible, and ever offerest to me something new to know, something new to love . . . and so on for eternity I shall ever be a little child beginning to be taught the rudiments of thy infinite divine nature. For thou art thyself the seat and centre of all good, and the only substance in this universe of shadows, and the heaven in which blessed spirits live and rejoice—Amen.

TO THE HOLY SPIRIT
Christina Rossetti
Nineteenth Century

As the wind is thy symbol
so forward our goings.
As the dove
so launch us heavenwards.
As water
so purify our spirits.
As a cloud
so abate our temptations.
As dew
so revive our languor.
As fire
so purge out our dross.

THY GREATNESS
Søren Kierkegaard
Nineteenth Century

God in Heaven, let me really feel my nothingness, not in order to despair over it, but in order to feel the more powerfully the greatness of Thy goodness.

THOU HAST LOVED US FIRST
Søren Kierkegaard

Father in Heaven! Thou hast loved us first, help us never to forget that Thou art love so that this sure conviction might triumph in our hearts over the seduction of the world, over the inquietude of the soul, over the anxiety for the future, over the fright of the past, over the distress of the moment. But grant also that this conviction might discipline our soul so that our heart might remain faithful and sincere in the love which we bear to all those whom Thou hast commanded us to love as we love ourselves.

WAKING
Søren Kierkegaard

Father in Heaven! When the thought of Thee wakes in our hearts let it not awaken like a frightened bird that flies about in dismay, but like a child waking from its sleep with a heavenly smile.

MY HEART
George Macdonald
Twentieth Century

Father, into thy hands I give the heart
Which left thee but to learn how good thou art.

A FOOL I BRING
George Macdonald

When I look back upon my life nigh spent,
Nigh spent, although the stream as yet flows on,
I more of follies than of sins repent,
Less for offence than love's shortcomings moan.
With self, O Father, leave me not alone—
Leave not with the beguiler the beguiled;
Besmirched and ragged, Lord, take back thine own:
A fool I bring thee to be made a child.

IN PRAISE OF THE NIGHT
Walter Rauschenbusch
Twentieth Century

    O Lord, we praise Thee for our sister, the Night, who folds all the tired folk of the earth in her comfortable robe of darkness and give them sleep. Release now the strained limbs of toil and smooth the brow of care. Grant us the refreshing draught of forgetfulness, that we may rise in the morning with a smile on our face. Comfort and ease those who toss wakeful on a bed of pain, or those aching nerves crave sleep and find it not. Save them from evil or despondent thoughts in the long darkness, and teach them so to lean on Thy all-pervading life and love, that their souls may grow tranquil and their bodies, too, may rest. And now, through Thee we send Good Night to all our brothers and sisters near and far, and pray for peace upon all the earth. Amen.

DISCERNMENT
Reinhold Niebuhr
Twentieth Century

O God, give us serenity to accept what cannot be changed, courage to change what should be changed, and wisdom to distinguish the one from the other.

PERSONAL PRAYERS

PERSONAL PRAYERS

PERSONAL PRAYERS

PERSONAL PRAYERS

AUTHOR INDEX

Abraham...7
Aquinas, Thomas...............................26
Augustine..23-24

Barnabas..21
Bernard of Clairvaux........................25
Bonaventura..26

Calvin, John...................................33-34
Clement of Alexandria....................21
Clement of Rome..............................20
Coverdale...30

Daniel..14
David...9
Donne, John.......................................35
Dying Thief..18

Francis of Assisi...........................26-27

Hannah...9

Ignatius of Loyola.............................30
Irenaeus..21

Jacob...8
Jeremiah...13
Jesus..15-16
John...17

Keble, John..37
Kierkegaard, Søren............................39

Luther, Martin...............................31-32

Macdonald, George..........................40
Melchizedek..7
Michelangelo......................................27
More, Thomas....................................29
Moses..8

Newman, John Henry..................37-38
Niebuhr, Reinhold.............................41

Paul..18-19
Peter..17
Publican..18

Rauschenbusch, Walter...................40
Rossetti, Christina.............................39

St. Patrick...25
Simeon..17
Solomon...9, 10
Stephen...18

Thomas à Kempis..............................28

Wesley, Charles..................................37
Wesley, John..................................36-37

SUBJECT INDEX

Blessing......................... 7, 10, 20, 30, 35

Charity..29
Comfort.............................11, 19, 28, 35
Complaint.................................... 13, 16

Dedication.....................9, 10, 16, 36, 40

Evening...33, 40

Faith..31, 32
Forgiveness.........................8, 9, 16, 18
Friends...28

Grace...29
Guidance........................... 8, 9, 13, 18,
         20, 21, 23, 24, 26, 27, 36, 41

High Priestly Prayer...........................15-16
Holiness...37
Holy Spirit..39
Hope...23

Intercession..7, 28

Knowledge of God.......................... 21, 39

Lament..................................... 12, 13, 16
Lord's Prayer.. 15

Love
  in community.. 30
  of Christ..18
  of God................................... 26, 29, 39

Mercy.................................... 18, 33, 40
Morning.. 22, 31

Obedience................................33, 34, 36

Peace....................................27, 32, 37
Petition................................8, 11, 16, 17,
              18, 19, 21, 23, 25, 31
Praise............ 10, 12, 14, 17, 19, 20, 24
Prayer.....................................29, 31, 37
Promise..8, 9

Relationship to Christ.....24, 26, 33, 28
Relationshp to God.........24, 35, 38, 39

Salvation...25
Service...23, 33, 36
Soul..12, 35, 37
Spirituality................................. 31, 36
Stewardship..21
Strength....................................... 18, 23

Thanksgiving......11, 14, 15, 22, 31, 36

Will of God..............................16, 30